FOGHORN LEGHORN

POEMS

BIG BRUISER DOPE BOY

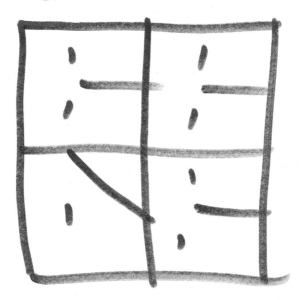

CL4SH

With total care I dedicate this book to all gay children.

CONTENTS

I BELIEVE IF YOU DON'T LIKE THIS BOOK, YOU SUCK

Foreword by Sam Pink

You are reading this book because you want new things. You want blood. You want to feel alive. You are trying to feed something. And the Dope Boy has chopped up his heart to hand out, thinking, 'There was too much of it anyway.'

The voice of this book. It has everything I want and yet I really can't explain it. It's hurt shit. A laugh that ends with a turned head and a teary eye. Each poem sings for lost unknowns to come home. It's funny, straightforward, absurd, sad, and, ultimately, true in the way that only art can be. More true than saying B comes after A. As true as handing someone your broken mask and just shrugging.

The Dope Boy came to Chicago for a couple days over the summer and hung out. He's a tall, brooding man. He dresses like a school shooter. His face always looks like a man making decisions in a war that might not be going his way. We played soccer in Millennium Park. We played darts. We walked around. We laughed.

But more importantly, he's a great man. He's an individual. He is a hunter of moods. He's my friend. And he has something to say. He's not here for crumbs, he's here to swipe them off the table and slam down his fist.

Say hello to the gay Rodney Dangerfield. Say hello to the Boom Doctor. Say hello to your first real boyfriend. Join me in welcoming this new voice. The Big Bruiser Dope Boy. One of the new wolves. May he forever huff and puff. We will never escape his cartoon.

INTERCOM

Please stay calm. Our crew is working on the
issue right now. Please stay seated with your
fingers crossed. I mean your seatbelt fastened.
I'm sorry. I don't know why I said that.
I'm not scared, and I'm running this thing, so
there's no reason why any of you should
be scared. We are all in this together.
This experience is a shared one, and
soon our bodies will be a shared one. Do
you know what I'm talking about? All of
us getting mixed in with one another,
like a party where soup is served, and we
are the soup that is being served, drinking
ourselves, everyone swallowed up at once.

YOU JUST GOT BOOMED

After S.S.

boom boom boom

you just got boomed

and I did it

I boomed you

you can call me the Boom Doctor

I have your emptied-out torso on the operating table

you are now living in a post-boom era, and

you want to assess the damages, but

seeing as you just got boomed, you no longer have the capacity to

your memory's composure, a trapdoor on a pirate ship

the pirates say "there's a traitor in our midst" and

massacre themselves, recognition overthrown

there fly your tall tales, away from you

far immeasurably away, a star behind a star behind a star

you want to put your finger on the source of the boom (me)

but your finger, split myriad from the tip, a limp squid hanging in the dark water

I'm sorry, did that hurt?

I didn't mean to hurt you, but

let's rewind the tape for old time's sake:

doom doom doom

I just got doomed

and you did it

you doomed me

take a look at those wondrous doom-magnets in action

ripping your wisdom teeth out while you try to make fun of the dentist through your sleep

your hypnotic calculator reciting the inanities of the sun

your language crawling through the bog, coated in cattails and mud

lost in the about-ness of it, submerged in the training room ice bath

your air bubbles floating up and popping at the surface like petty apologies

while I watch with absurd patience your death-defying approximation:

the invisible man, dressed in bandages that you unravel and wind yourself into

betraying me with your newness

you give me a bum (w)rap, make me look like a mistake

don't worry, shatter-eyes, your time will come

has come, is come

you can call me the Welcome Mat

you can call this the door

the wall between us goes boom, and

our heart fills the house

do you remember feeling vulnerable

when you thought you saw me coming, the

ancient, blurred look on my face?

I thought I saw a hollow look on yours

GAINING BACK THE UPPER HAND

I'm not a criminal. I'm a prison.
I incubate transgression. Duck duck goose.
More like duck duck duck, ad infinitum.
I stay ducking geese—supremely lucky.
Dry shit is just ash. We burn our food from
the inside out. Bile weasels into sky.
I'm saying everything old. A cellar
janitor, hang a mirror facedown from
the roof and I'll smear heaven with sewage.
Outer space has abandonment issues.
The latest plague received a damning score
on an aptitude test. What's news to God?
Let's catch the apocalypse with its pants
down, make it suck on our hot soft plastic.

AN EXCITING NIGHT (I'M AFRAID IT MADE ME WANT TO DO MORE)

When my mom called and said her dad's health was
failing fast, that we'd be leaving early
the next morning to drive 1200 miles
to her hometown in Wisconsin, I was
high on coke at a friend's birthday party.
I wanted to go back home right then, but
I was so high. I told a room full of
people, some of whom I didn't know, that
my grandfather was dying. I put on
a song and the person whose birthday it
was said, "This is too sad," and turned it off.
Did I snort coke after I found out, though?
I don't think I did, but can't say for sure.
While we were gone, a bunch of her plants died.

69 REMAKES (PART 1/3)

Remake of *The Matrix* that's security cam footage of me drunkenly breaking into a Best Buy and passing out with a VR headset on.

Remake of *Memento* where I'm stoned in a room trying to remember what I was talking about.

Remake of *Batman* where I walk around at night in a cheap mask hitting cops in their ribs and shins with a bat while shrieking dementedly.

Remake of *Life of Pi* where I fall off the raft and drown in the first 5 minutes and the rest of the movie is a 2-hour shot of the ocean.

Remake of *Bloodsport* where I spend an hour and a half trying to do the splits and rip open my taint and bleed out on a gymnastics mat.

Remake of *Say Anything* where I show up uninvited at

my father's funeral holding a boombox over my head playing "Hippa to da Hoppa" by Ol' Dirty Bastard.

Remake of *Man on Fire* where I return to my old high school, self-immolate with kerosene, and, bellowing madly, tackle my football coach.

Remake of *Home Alone* where I break into my dad's house, hide in his bed with a knife, and, when he finds me, calmly say, "tuck me in, motherfucker."

Remake of *Top Gun* where the gun is at the bottom.

Remake of *Speed* where I give out weed and brandy on a Megabus, incite a riot, and drive it off an overpass into a sports stadium during a game.

Remake of *The Running Man* where I intercept my dad during his morning jog and chase him down the street with a knife.

Remake of *The Deer Hunter* where I, wearing a large deer hide, hold my dad hostage and force him to play Russian roulette with me.

Remake of *Die Hard* where I am, until I meet death's all-forgiving embrace, haunted by the undying memory of the time I met Bruce Willis.

Remake of *Homeward Bound* where the pets eat the family when they get back because they turned feral and are starving to death.

Remake of *The Mighty Ducks* about strong ducks.

Remake of *Air Bud* where, in the last seconds of the final game, the CIA assassinates the dog because it's actually a Russian spy.

Remake of *Commando* where I attend a gun show wearing nothing but a camouflage jockstrap and buy every gun there to "assassinate my ass."

Remake of *Little Miss Sunshine* where I skip around a Whole Foods wearing nothing but a diaper drooling and playing a ukulele and toy xylophone.

Remake of *The Lion King* called *The Truthin' King* about a king who doesn't lie.

Remake of *Gone with the Wind* where I leave with the wind.

Remake of *3 Ninjas* where I accost three boys on a sidewalk and demand they karate chop me to death.

Remake of *3 Ninjas Kick Back* where I, wearing casts and wrapped in bandages, accost three boys on a sidewalk and demand they kick me to death.

Remake of *3 Ninjas Knuckle Up* where I am visited in the hospital by three boys and, barely able to speak, I say, "finish it, you pussies."

LENGTHENING THE STORM OR
HOW TO BE BELIEVABLY FRAGILE

Fit as many fingers as you can
inside the gaping hole of my
rhetoric. I mean it—really stretch out that ass-
umptive void. It won't hurt me, or I won't act
hurt, unless you expect me to,
in which case I'll compete
for the affection of algorithms
against my peers, who climb
pine trees, which makes this swaying
and yowling in the wind in the name
of ghosts I'm doing a little explicable,
and when I say a little, I mean
a Chicken Little. I say *The sky is falling,*
but mean I'm falling through the sky like rain.
I'm doing this on purpose says
the textile factory collapse. *I didn't mean
to hurt you* says the hippo, child in jaw—
contorted pomegranate. They tell

the truth, which is why it makes
little sense to anybody other than chickens
with their heads cut off, doing what they know best.

And here we are
on the other side of the electric fence,
barbed snotty weeds
sprouting from the cracked ground,
people in passing cars
not thinking to notice us, and even if they did,
we wouldn't be enough for them to pull over
and stare—advancing along the highway,
its inbuilt purpose, hearing static chew
pop songs on the radio
like lumps of gum with dirt in them, gazing through
frames grayed by runny splays
of what were once shiny flying bugs.

Falling through the sky, by grace
I grabbed to a tiny rickety wing
of a single engine Cessna
that, after bending loud tight loops
above a dispassionate reptilian crowd, landed
on a desolate bow of road in the waste. But the sky—
the sky keeps falling through me
without landing, like a shadow that can't
find the floor. Maybe, if you fit a dry hand
inside me, you can cease this hysteria, or at least
I won't be so wet and swift. Maybe, if you fit
yourself inside me, I'll run out of air
to talk with, and I'll rest for the first time

since you showed at the door
I don't live behind anymore. You'll turn around
and get in your car, and I'll be in the
passenger seat, unconscious and under
your care, like I've been this entire time—just faking
wakefulness. What we have is special. To the rest
of the world (where soon we'll be) we look
like mutes, like rain before it hits, before it's no longer
rain.

GAY RODNEY DANGERFIELD

I tell ya it's hard going to the movies when you're gay, ya know? I took my straight 14-year-old nephew, whose favorite comedian is Amy Schumer, to see her new movie, *I Feel Pretty*. I, on the other hand, being gay, had to see *I Feel Pretty Gay*.

I tell ya it's hard going grocery shopping when you're gay, ya know? The other day I went to Trader Joe's and accidentally ended up penetrating two pistachio mochis I'd squeezed together and forgot weren't butt cheeks.

I tell ya I get no respect as a deeply repressed gay man, ya know? Why, just the other day I was making love to the superimposed, mentally projected image of my old man on top of my wife's face and I said, "Say 'good job' when I cum." S/he told me I should only take pride in my work!

I tell ya it's hard getting a driver's license when you're gay, ya know? Just the other day I was getting mine renewed and the DMV clerk asked if I was an organ donor. "It's not the kind of donation where you get to keep it after you pull it out of his asshole," he added.

I tell ya I get no respect as a severely closeted gay man, ya know? Just the other day I was driving my yellow Nissan Xterra to buy a cup of gorilla taint flavored fro-yo. This guy in a way less cool car than mine cut me off. Needless to say I lost my appetite and had sex with him.

I tell ya it's hard having parents when you're gay, ya know? When I came out to my mom, she had to deal with both the disappointment of me never having children in a heterosexual marriage, and even worse, the crushing let down of knowing I'd never have sex with her again.

I tell ya it's hard being a hopelessly closeted gay man married to a woman with three children, ya know? I want to tell them the truth, but if I did, it would tear my family apart, not to mention my asshole.

I tell ya it's hard getting a car wash when you're a tyrannized queer, ya know? It took everything in me to refuse the "clear coat" I wanted but couldn't afford.

I tell ya it's hard eating pizza when you're gay, ya know? Why, if my memory serves me well, it was just the other night that I ordered a thin crust sausage and green bell pepper pizza. I had the worst acid reflux that night. It's hard enough burning at one end!

I tell ya it's hard watching *Will & Grace* when you're gay, ya know? It's almost like the characters' homosexuality being consistently used for punchlines your family laughs at in their "acceptance" of you makes you feel somehow even more ashamed and less like an individual.

HOLOGRAM BABY

Baby I'm a disposable camera.

Baby you stop me dead in my tracks, burn a hole in my brain.

Baby I'm your biggest fan, I'm wearing your t-shirt, can't you read the pop-calligraphy?—can't you recognize your own handwriting?

Baby I've got filing cabinets full of dreams you wrote, my office is dripping with dream-juice, my hands are holding fresh dollar bills, ready to spend on you.

Baby you make it all seem worthwhile, you get me out of bed in the morning, you make the coffee taste hopeful, you make me leave the house with confidence and go to the office where I fill cabinets with dreams of you.

Baby take these handcuffs off of me, now put them back on.

Baby your picture exposes the end of what I desire, which is the beginning of what I desire, a road paved in dreams.

Baby the cacti are singing me road directions.

Baby I'm confused, the world is changing—quick, tell me something I can trust for even a second because I can't come up with anything good.

Baby stop hiding in the utility closet.

Baby stop looking like an angel.

Baby don't open your mouth, don't ruin the suspense we've worked so hard to sustain.

Baby my hair is standing on end, my nerves scrambling to catch up with you, playing possum in the moonlight.

Baby the wise know their foolishness well.

Baby you were cast in bronze, racing headlong toward me through a hot glass tunnel.

Baby the glass is cracking, you're humming in my ears like a flute.

Baby thinking of you like this is a holy tradition at
this point.

Baby I see you across the room at the party, I can't hear
you, but from the look on your face I can tell what you're
talking about—you're talking about finding the disease
in me.

Baby the world is hungry and so are we, but we're harm-
less enough you and I—tadpoles in a puddle of tears.

Baby you may be my baby but I feel just like a child when
it comes to you, I'm trying to stay warm in the nest
you built.

Baby puke inside my mouth, tell me something I can
strap my heart to with a horse-hide belt.

Baby fire is quiet and painless and ice is a punishing
screech in the wild.

Baby our bodies are being destroyed and I can't turn my
eyes away from you.

Baby I'm sorry for being dramatic but the world, inexplic-
able and cancerous, moves like an insect across the
ceiling.

Baby was that you on the side of a building, riding a
golden wagon in the sunset?

Baby I hope I'm right on target, hope I'm reaching you clear.

Baby are you tuned in?—is this making any sense?

Baby our kingdom has epilepsy, we live in a sensitive fortress, we might have to smuggle ourselves out in disguise to survive.

Baby you're just over this hill, just around this corner, just through this door, I can see your shadow hinting safety from where I stand, I'll follow the necessary logical steps.

Baby we're ruthless when we talk to each other, do we really believe it's fun to drag this cruel contest out?

Baby I have to go to the bathroom, if you don't have an excuse to shut your eyes I'd be glad to give you one if it'll help, because baby, I'm here to help.

Baby we are commas in each other's breaths, hitches in each other's steps.

Baby we only want to feel what we heard feels good.

Baby let's put on the rubber gloves and go on a rampage, we'll have the town talking for weeks.

Baby gossip flings off of us effortlessly: all we do is tell ourselves stories, we're a force to be reckoned with.

Baby what are we doing now?—let's find another problem we can't solve.

Baby you remind me I'm not yet finished with the task at hand, your tent glowing on the mountainside, I can smell the smoke from the meadow below.

Baby I'll be there soon, don't fall asleep yet, it's cold, I'll make my way up the mountain in the dark.

Baby I have no way of knowing what I've done, I'm walking to you without a person to count on.

98 DOLLARS

While working
Smoking a cigarette outside the bar
That I bummed from my boss Tom
A gay couple I served earlier
It is a gay bar after all
Comes walking down the sidewalk
Side by side, I don't know
Where they went

But they are back now
Smiling at me sitting in
An orange plastic chair
In light rain, two other
Presumably straight guys
Come walking the other way

As they pass one of the gay guys
Says something flirtatious

To the straight guys
His boyfriend turns to me and says
"Can you see why I love him?"

I say no I can't see why
And don't see how anyone
Other than he can see why
He loves him

He says "ah, you've
Outsmarted me"
I didn't say this but
I didn't outsmart him
I didn't out anything him

After closing walking home
Raining harder now
I see
A man asleep under a storefront awning
His head on his shoes

A woman asleep under a church arch
Her belongings around her body

Outside a dive close by my house
Torn up playing cards
From an abandoned three-card Monte game

I don't know why someone
Loves someone

I don't know why
The jackal fails

I don't see how I
Can ever fall asleep
Just like that

I made 98 dollars in tips tonight
My housemate let me in through the kitchen
In the basement because I forgot to
Bring my keys when I left

I was lucky he was still up

DEVIL BOTTOMLESS

I'm being discovered by the historians a thousand years
from now and they're not impressed.

I'm digging a hole, squandering every last piece of
darkness.

I'm in bed with the phone held close while the Devil
dreams to me on the other end of the line, swings his
pocket-watch in front of my face in flashes, pours
gunpowder in my ears with a funnel, which is his mouth,
and camouflages himself into tired pictures of the earth.

I'm mesmerized and seized by the trembling fist of his
visions.

I don't remember him, but I remember what he told me,
and now I say it like he said it, like a lie being emptied
of form.

A lie is something clever enough to allow.

To allow a lie is to sneak the Truth away from yourself for as long as you can bear the work.

It's never again, forever.

Always like this, a rotten baby.

I'm instant gone excited in the grave.

It doesn't work.

I've dissected the world as small as I can and have wrapped everything in bacon.

Space is fat with the prospect of purpose and grossly incomplete.

I'm taking deep breaths of stones.

I'm looking through a man who's looking at a man trying to say something about himself, where he stands, what accounts for what, how he got this grotesque, who it was that pinned him down in the night and forced on him a story to live by, something to help him move more easily, a physical clue, instructions and explanations that suggest who he is and what makes the inside cough on the outside, that there's a difference, that there's a secret to know, that the organs

are doors that transport the miraculous and
commonplace.

When he tries to make things simple, they become
complicated, when he tries to make anything into
anything, it becomes nothing at the same time.

The harder he looks at it, the harder it looks to him.

I'm discovering my cadaver a thousand years from now
and it looks nothing like me.

I look nothing like me.

My eyes look like an incoming snowstorm.

My look looks like a man in a coma whose flesh is on fire
and he's stinking up the whole room and all is lost, and
lost begins again and so do I.

Magician the tailor measuring dreams dramatic.

Ark of wound massive hemorrhaging memory taking
drunken soldiers hostage, bathing in terror, laughing in
green and red valleys and cheeks.

Bone blinks.

Action negatives.

Devil face.

Scream forever.

Remember his song.

Forget what it sounds like.

Last thing you hear is wind blowing clear through the vastest canyon.

Last thing you feel is heat.

Last thing you think is chains.

Last thing you are is life.

69 REMAKES (PART 2/3)

Remake of 3 *Ninjas: High Noon at Mega Mountain* where Hulk Hogan and I are a gay married couple raising three wonderful boys.

Remake of *Baby's Day Out* where I crawl across a metro area licking people's calves.

Remake of *Dances with Wolves* where I lead a pack of wolves wearing leather jackets into a dance club and we do a really cool dance routine.

Remake of *Child's Play* about an elementary school-aged playwright.

Remake of *Honey, I Shrunk the Kids* where I shrink myself and shoot myself out of a BB gun back into my mother's uterus.

Remake of *Saturday Night Fever* where I sit alone in a basement in a kiddie pool filled with ice water.

Remake of *Adventures in Babysitting* where my babysitter gives me a blowjob.

Remake of *Predator* where my babysitter gets charged with sexual assault after giving me a blowjob.

Remake of *It* where I dress up like a clown and crawl down a sewer drain to look for my childhood.

Remake of *Good Will Hunting* where I walk into a bar and double jump kick both Ben Affleck and Matt Damon in their chests with steel-toe boots.

Remake of *Big Trouble in Little China* where my asshole, affectionately nicknamed "Little China," gets gaped by a guy named "Skirt Rustle."

Remake of *Every Which Way But Loose* where I get revenge on "Skirt Rustle" by crushing his hand bones in the grip of my extremely tight asshole.

Remake of *Mannequin* where I con my way into the conceptual art world by driving a remote control motorcycle with a mannequin on it through MoMA.

Remake of *Mission: Impossible* where I retrieve a free slice of pizza from a visiting writer reception without interacting with anyone.

Remake of *Silver Linings Playbook* where I enter a break-dancing competition and, attempting a shoulder roll, break my neck.

Remake of *The Wolf of Wall Street* where a wolf who can

smell how rich people are stalks Wall Street biting throats in descending order.

Sequel to *Big* called *Small* where I get turned into a prepubescent with the same mind as I have now and kill myself.

Remake of *Finding Forrester* where Bob Dylan stabs a basketball with a switchblade and, chain-smoking, beats Haruki Murakami in a marathon.

Remake of *Jaws* that's a "character study" of Jaws from the James Bond movies where he's suffering from clinical depression.

Remake of *Can't Hardly Wait* called *Can't Softly Wait* where a waiter goes to boot camp to learn how to be a tough waiter.

Remake of *Jumanji* where I squat in a mansion for a year and master a Robin Williams impression, then lead a stampede thru the SF Bay Area.

Remake of *Flight of the Navigator* where I break into a Tesla, hide, and, when discovered by the owner(s), say, "take me home with you."

Remake of *Billy Elliot* about a boy who, growing up in a culture where all boys are expected to become ballet dancers, wants to be a professional boxer.

150 DOLLARS

Sunday at the bar it's dead I'm
the only person there until an
old fat guy comes in

sits down and orders a Coke
says he's from Chicago just
passing through

seeing if he can find college
guys to sell him their
underwear

I say "oh yeah? how much do
you pay for them?"
he says "50 dollars usually

and 100 dollars
if they piss or come on them"

it's dead at the bar so I say
"sure but I'm not in college
and I'm not wearing underwear

I'm wearing a jockstrap"
he says "that's okay could you piss
on it a little?"

I say "I don't have to piss
but give me 5 minutes"
I go into the back area of the bar

by the walk-in cooler
and remove my boots then jeans
and jockstrap then put back on my

jeans then boots and walk over to
the sink where there is a bottle of
Trader Joe's hand lotion

I press down on the pump squirting
a quarter-sized amount of lotion
into the palm of my hand

I go to the women's bathroom
because it has a lock
one of those rudimentary locks

where a hook attached to the door

goes in a hoop attached to the frame
I masturbate to my reserve

of go-to images and situations
and am able to come quite fast
which surprises me

I forgot I could come so fast
because when masturbating for pleasure
I tend to prolong and savor it

when in this case I am providing a service
I feel proud that I have that kind of control
to come under pressure and expectation

and to deliver a product promptly
I step out of the bathroom smiling
and hand the old fat guy the jockstrap

"here you go"
he lifts the jockstrap
presses it into his face and inhales deeply

through his nose and exhales
through his mouth saying "oh yeah
could you show me your dick?"

I say "I really can't at the bar I'm working"
he says "can I feel your dick through your jeans?
I'll give you 50 more dollars"

I say "okay sure" and for a minute
he feels my dick through my jeans
with his hand squeezing it

while holding the underwear to his face
I get anxious and bored and say "okay
I have to get back to work"

he hands me 150 dollars and says "thank you"
I say "sure"
after a while he finishes his Coke and leaves

later about 30 minutes until the end of my shift
the old fat guy walks back in
sits down and orders a Coke

I prepare the bar
for the next person to work
I clock out and as I'm leaving say

"bye" to the old fat guy
and he says quietly
"are you interested

in earning any more money?"
I say "no"
he says nervously as if to avert

making a scene "okay no problem
no problem"

CRAB CAKE

Do not discuss the raking of our fin-
gers through our hair to lubricate our scalps
with oil from pores that seep in gaps of anx-
ious thoughts bewildered by a certitude
we ideate as having been detached
from us, but listen here, if you can find
that home from which you left, that birth, that for-
gone memory itself, that sheath of na-
da that ejected you in plasmic ex-
position when you sensed without homun-
cular ablation, rot, and did not know
what was not known and bore no images.
Don't move, don't moan, don't look for what you are
already. Light is death the fastest way.

DISPERSING ANXIETY

dispersing anxiety by imagining ripping off your own
nipples and shoving them in your ears like ear plugs after
hearing a person talk in that vacuous "using big words to
sound smart but not talking about anything" way for over
a minute

cartoonishly spraying them in the face with your nipple
blood, collapsing to the ground with two dark red holes in
your chest, smiling, hearing nothing but the reserve of
blood leave your head, the exiting warmth

you die, then come back as that person, talking,
surrounded by giant open human mouths moving up
and down

as that person, you stop talking, and the mouths frown

"good," you say

as that person, you jump really hard toward a vacant baby stroller and transform midair into a baby before you land

as that baby, you shit yourself and fall asleep

you wake up pushing the stroller off a parking garage and into an alleyway dumpster four stories below

"goodnight," you say, "now you truly have nothing to prove"

you jump off the parking garage and, as you fall, you see the baby's sleeping open mouth; you shrink to the size of a coin and fall into it

you wake up choking and cough a quarter into my palm

I'm rich now, so I don't need to talk

CHAT COMPRESSION

Genuflect down the Eustachian tube of
your own neuroatypicality.
Everyone's lives as inside one-liners.
Nothing is funny. I laugh all the time.
The currency is bad science fiction.
Dead mammal gazes only aspiring to
zombiehood. Crypts packed with stuffed animals
all lonely for me. Blow a stale kiss to
the redemption paradigm, enter the
Sad Real Now, where your own mother sees the
waste of flesh you are. Orgasms of deep
identification. Haunted shitmode.
The big diapers of understanding, in
the cheap air conditioning they're preserved.

BOYS

It could, I suppose, in theory, be plau-
sible, but, despite the desirabil-
ity of my milkshake, would I really
want *all* the boys in the yard? The wild ho-
moeroticism of everyday
life. The NFL seems like the propa-
ganda wing of the US militar-
y. American football games are com-
mercials for corporate proxy wars. The
way cocaine makes straight guys give candid, un-
solicited, detailed accounts of their
relationships with their dads. Saying, "I
can become anything," before veering
into oncoming traffic. "Veiled," not "wild."

MRS. DOUBTFIRE 2

Mrs. Doubtfire 2, forever wandering the corridors of would-be genius.

Epiphanies pulled from us just before the moment of awakening.

Mrs. Doubtfire 2, in which Sally Field peels back the flesh of her own visage, only to reveal the face of Mrs. Doubtfire beneath.

In which Mrs. Doubtfire hitches a ride on an errant drone, face flapping, shouting "Haloooo" at the top of her voice—pan out to the silent desert.

In which Mrs. Doubtfire immolates a group of voice-over actors with a flamethrower. "My first day as a woman and I'm already getting hot flashes."

In which Mrs. Doubtfire sodomizes Pierce Brosnan in a vicious pantomime of the Heimlich maneuver as Harvey Fierstein rubs his eyes with cayenne.

In which the cobra hood of Harvey Fierstein unfurls. In which Harvey Fierstein spits venom.

I think we'll have to go to the next level: latex.

In which Brosnan's spent viscera leaks out as Mrs. Doubtfire walks off. "I don't work with the males, 'cause I used to be one."

In which Sally Field plays *Jumanji* with Bonnie Hunt. In which Sally Field is hit by a Guinness truck. It was the drink that killed her. It was a run-by fruiting. It was David Alan Grier in the parlor with the candlestick.

Mr. Hillard, do you consider yourself humorous?

In which the little girl from *Matilda*'s mouth fills with blood.

In which the little girl from *Matilda* appears in the dark at your bedside at 3am, whispering: sink the sub hide the weasel park the porpoise a bit of the old humpty dumpty little jack horny the horizontal mambo, hmm? The bone dancer Rumpleforeskin baloney bop a bit of the old cunning linguistics.

I am Job.

Do you speak English?

I am Job.

In which Mrs. Doubtfire eats a salad made from the toes of babies and Mercedes hood ornaments while singing "Dude Looks Like A Lady." In which Steven Tyler peels back the flesh of his own visage to reveal Steven Tyler as Mrs. Doubtfire in *Jumanji*.

In which the faces of women are collected in jars. I'm ready for my close-up, Mr. Demille.

In which Matthew Lawrence melts like a sno-cone in Phoenix as the theme song from Blossom plays on a loop. Nanu Nanu.

In which Mrs. Doubtfire peels back the flesh of her own visage only to reveal the face of Sally Field as Bonnie Hunt in *Jumanji*.

In which Mrs. Doubtfire is only certain about flames.

In which I must look like a yeti in this get-up.

In which Mr. Sprinkles the mailman knocks on the door and Mrs. Doubtfire answers. "Oh, a big knock on the door! Who could it be and do we have enough time?"

"Mr. Sprinkles, boys and girls! Hello Mr. Sprinkles!"

In which Mr. Sprinkles the mailman peels back the flesh of his own visage only to reveal a glass face containing a diorama of Mrs. Doubtfire opening the door to find Mr. Sprinkles, as marionette, peeling back the flesh of his own visage only to reveal Mrs. Doubtfire.

In which Mrs. Doubtfire, deep sea in a bathyscaphe, tele-pathically encounters a narwhal. Kill me, it entreats her. I have a horn which contains the ache of men's bile, the accumulation of the moment an arm is poised to hurl a harpoon. The moment of baleen. The moment of Mrs. Doubtfire peeling back the flesh of her own visage only to reveal a smoldering pile of auks. I am somehow the unicorn of the sea. How is that possible? "Oh no dear, I think they've outlawed whaling."

In which Mrs. Doubtfire follows the Ho Chi Minh Trail, follows the Ho Chi Minh Trail.

In which the eyes of children in a room tear up simulta-neously, dioramas of the ocean. An old woman is walking from their house for the last time. She knows this.

All my love to you, poppet, you're going to be alright. Bye-bye.

SUPER BOWL IN REVERSE

I'm going to Disneyland—one, two, three.
The Magic Kingdom needs Prince Violent
whose helmet hosts plunderous alphabets,
trades the chariots in for fighter jets.
Coliseum box seats hate to see Moors
joyous, prefer respectability,
would rather them not celebrate, have class,
be grateful, march solemn to locker rooms,
give back to their communities, because
owners won't—Space Mountain morality,
stadium lights military grade, "We
have you surrounded. Leave with your hands down."
Remember, we made you—a father-like
nutritional supplement. You owe us.

GOLDEN TRIANGLE, SETX

After J.R.

platinum feathers gleam beneath the mire;
refinery smog warps hunter orange;
hydrocracker unbraids cotton wreckage,
splits wax into clouds, beards the firmament;
birds dance, blood wings; cancer masks, silver lungs;
pus eyes, tallow systems; nauseous hatred,
ringing out; toxic shapes, sad histories;
family, friends, lovers; distorted, gone;
daddies cook venison gumbo in huts;
assault rifles bordering Walden Swamp;
gasoline plumes, iridescent Copa;
bone flocks, mist dome, emerges Realnesstree;
we wear this world that wears on us so that
it passes over us, misses itself

WALKING THROUGH

we were staying at your friend's place
a small apartment up two long stairways
while he was gone

we had a flight that evening
we had recently come back from walking around
you asked me if I wanted to smoke

I said yes
you told me to make sure the door wasn't locked
or to not shut the door behind me if it was

you walked out the door, down the hall
and out another door to the fire escape
I followed you, shutting the door behind me

I joined you on the highest platform of the fire escape
from where we could look down into the gutters

you said you didn't lock the door, did you?

I went to the door and wasn't able to turn the locked knob
I looked back at you
you thought I was joking

or were hoping I was
but could tell I wasn't
I put my hands in my hair, cursed and apologized

I said I thought it wasn't locked
I locked the knob out of habit when I came in and forgot
what are we going to do?

we left our wallets inside, your phone inside
my phone was in my pocket, but it was about to die
you tried to finesse the door open

said fuck it and kicked the door
the sound of wood splitting
we got in

now the door was broken
the area around the latch was cracked, splintered, bulging
the deadbolt was fine

I unscrewed the strike plate from the side of the door
different pieces leapt out
and tinkled onto the floor

we looked up videos to figure out how to repair it

then gave up after about an hour and a half
of trying to hold the unfamiliar metal pieces and springs
in place

while shoving them in the hole
we had to be at the airport in a few hours
I called a locksmith

he showed up and told us the latch was shot
bent from kicking in the door
repair wasn't possible, only replacement

he left to get a new latch
while you left to get us lunch
while I stayed and waited for the locksmith

you got back and we ate on the front steps
the locksmith came back
installed a new latch in the brittle, damaged hole

we left, bought glue, came back
I squeezed the door as it dried
we had sex in the bathroom

shared a cigarette looking
across the balmy city, tops of other houses
the sky turning soft around bridge lights

we made the airport without issue
had what we told ourselves were our last cigarettes
outside the terminal next to flight attendants

we fixed the door, or got it fixed together
your friend won't find out
until——unless——you tell him (you should)

when you said it felt like we were doomed from the start
I thought that was cheap
what doesn't look doomed, walking through its ruins?

I got a message from the future today
it told me not to bother
but I wasn't here to hear it

69 REMAKES (PART 3/3)

Remake of *Dog Day Afternoon* where I rob a bank and adopt 500 dogs who I train to "crowd surf" me everywhere on their backs in a roving horde.

Remake of *Escape from New York* where I live my entire life without ever traveling to New York.

Remake of *Heavyweights* where a group of healthy children get sent by their parents to a summer camp designed to make them morbidly obese.

Remake of *Daddy Day Care* where all the kids die because the dads don't know what they're doing/aren't really dads/just named the daycare that.

Remake of *The Saint* where Val Kilmer gets locked in a padded room in a straitjacket, yet he continues to perform various disguises, voices.

Remake of *The Indian in the Cupboard* called *The Dad in*

the Cabinet where I find a tiny version of my dad in my kitchen cabinet and eat him.

Remake of *Tremors* where I attempt to wean myself off an alcohol habit without having a seizure/dying from withdrawals.

Remake of *Marley & Me* called *Charlie & Me* where I marry Charles Manson, break him out of prison, and we move to Alaska to train sled dogs.

Remake of *American Beauty* where the American public admits to themselves that they adored Kevin Spacey precisely because he's a creepy pedo twink chaser.

Remake of *They Live* where the guy puts on the special sunglasses but it just shows him the wounded, spoiled child at the core of a bunch of people.

2nd Remake of *Die Hard* where I spend Christmas Eve barefoot in an abandoned building drinking champagne and listening to Sade with Reginald VelJohnson.

Remake of *Mr. Smith Goes to Washington* where I try to pass a law that makes cutting a loaf of bread unevenly punishable by death.

Remake of *Psycho* where I dress up like my mother (I don't kill anyone, I just flawlessly dress up like my mother and lead, dressing up like my mother in a manner that aspires to exact replication aside, a plain life).

Remake of *Father of the Bride* called *Father of the Side*

where the father of an engaged man's mistress eats beans and franks alone in a small apartment.

Remake of *Lord of the Rings* where I spend the remainder of my days mastering the art of ring juggling, bringing direct joy to thousands of children across the globe, never to read Tolkien's trilogy.

Remake of *What Women Want* called *What Asses Want* where I gain the ability to telepathically eavesdrop on the surprisingly sentient and discursive interior monologues of various asses and learn, through the false security of their private candor, they're not too pleased with me!

Remake of *The Graduate* where, whether I graduate or not, I'll be 55K in debt and be qualified for the same jobs as I was before I earned (or didn't) a BA in writing and literature.

Remake of *George of the Jungle* where, walking through a rainforest, I encounter George Saunders crouched on the ground wearing a safari hat (turns out he's tripping balls and communicating with insects, snakes, lemurs, etc.)

Remake of *Brokeback Mountain* where I deeply inhale the faint but unmistakable scent of my perished lover through the fabric of his left-behind denim jacket, and, jumping off a mountain in a flying wingsuit to spread his ashes, I break my back.

Remake of *There's Something About Mary* I unwittingly participated in when this guy I dated wore my cum in his beard to the bar after servicing me.

Remake of *Altered States* where I lock myself in a room and force myself to watch 10 Steven Seagal movies in a row taking 2 hits of LSD/2 hours.

Remake of *True Lies* where I get in the wet concrete-filled hole with the nuclear warhead draped in the USA flag and give a *Terminator 2: Judgement Day* style thumbs-up.

Remake of *Click* where I point the magic remote control at earth and press "off."

YOUR FIRST REAL BOYFRIEND

I'm going to be your first real boyfriend

I'm going to show you the meaning of suffering

I'm going to show you how to love another man

How to shower him with love and urine

I'm going to be your first real love

I'm going to break your shell by breaking my shell on your shell

I'm going to chisel away at that monster

I'm going to make rage funny

Your boyfriend will frown

I'm going to attack you with patience and imagination

For every thing I say, there are ten things I don't say

I'm going to torture you with the knowledge that I think
you're worthy of a robust love

For every thing I write, there are hidden cities of animals
living in complex, yet unaware systems of bunkers under
domestic objects, mating and killing

I'm going to show you the meaning of romance

I don't know the meaning of romance

That is romance

Your boyfriend will write to you in a conversational tone
he doesn't think of as poetry

I'm going to be your first real engagement with poetry

I'm going to show you how to make a world that isn't a
Walt Disney World, or a World of Warcraft

I'm going to show you how to let loose and be fun and
social

I'm not going to do that

Your boyfriend will neither lie nor cheat

Your first real boyfriend

I'm going to be your father and your son at the same time

AWARD SPEECH

There are going to be people
along the way who will try to
inoculate you with patronizing
counsel. You should feign
gratitude, thank them for their
guidance, then run away, because
they are tormented and need you
as an object of their help in order
to locate power in their shrunken
sense of might. They will throw
darts in the dark at a thing called
"you." Honey, they are talking
about themselves. First, I would
like to thank God for
empowering me to not fall prey
to the agendas of these phony
motherfuckers. Speculation will
be made concerning your

motivation. You don't have to
bare wilderness to any hungry
strategy. Just say, "You'll have
to feel this way on your own."
You'll be dead by the time your
letter arrives. Like a vial of
poison with your name on it, the
conceit of any onlooker will be
slipped in a drink your mouth
will be too cremated to address.
This is so unexpected. I'm
rambling; I'm speechless. I'm
going viral as I gyrate the gospel.
As with the music at your
funeral, you will be escorted
offstage by the limits of
sentimentality. You will be
saying something different, but
the village will be busy burning
itself down. For those I've
forgotten to mention, you know
who you are, and I thank you for
your guidance. Let the spectral
orgy now obscure the acid
issuing from my muscles drunk
on hell. I'm honored and
humbled to even be included in
the category of Best Liar among
these amazing, talented liars.
This is for you. My children are
my heroes, obviously, but you all

are my war heroes, you just don't
know it yet. See if you can see
my eyes through the smoke.
There's so much more work to be
done, but we've come a long way
from feeling right in the world.

ACKNOWLEDGMENTS

Grateful acknowledgment is made to the editors of the publications in which the poems in this book originally appeared (some in different form and under different titles):

Burningword: "Hologram Baby"; *Deluge*: "An Exciting Night (I'm Afraid It Made Me Want to Do More)," "Award Speech," "Lengthening the Storm or How to Be Believably Fragile," "Super Bowl in Reverse"; *Fanzine*: "Crab Cake"; *Fluland*: "69 Remakes"; *Hobart*: "You Just Got Boomed"; *New York Tyrant Magazine*: "Your First Real Boyfriend"; *Philosophical Idiot*: "Walking Through"; *Tragickal*: "Mrs. Doubtfire 2"; *Witch Craft Magazine*: "Intercom"; *Word Riot*: "Devil Bottomless"

With gratitude to Bill Martin, Joey Russo, Patrick Welsh, Sam Pink, Sean Kilpatrick, Elizabeth Ellen, Aaron Burch, Steve Anwyll, Cowboy Roland, Leza Cantoral, Christoph Paul, Bhanu Kapil, Junior Burke, Andrew Schelling, Reed Bye, Anne Waldman, Giancarlo DiTrapano, Jordan Castro, Elle Nash, Ctch Bsnss, Paul Cunningham, Brandon Diehl, Kat Giordano, Tex Avery, Mel Blanc, Rodney Dangerfield, Norm Macdonald, Jean Genet, Oscar Wilde, Thom Gunn, Richard Siken, Gus Van Sant, Harmony Korine, Robin Williams, Beatrice Arthur, lysergic acid diethylamide, psilocybin, cannabis, WOOF'S Madison, R&R Lounge Denver, Nasty Pig, Gun Oil, Brian Hess, and my mother.

ABOUT THE AUTHOR

Big Bruiser Dope Boy has been writing for ten years. This is his first book. He lives in Colorado. He tweets @bigbruiserdopeb.

CL⊲SH

WE PUT THE LIT IN LITERARY

CLASHBOOKS.COM
yesclash.com

Twitter, IG,Facebook @CLASHBooks

Email: clashmediabooks@gmail.com